COMMON CORE CLINICS

Grade 5

Mathematics

Measurement, Data, and Geometry

Common Core Clinics, Mathematics, Measurement, Data, and Geometry, Grade 5
OT322 / 414NA

ISBN: 978-0-7836-8496-3

Author: Rebecca Motil
With special thanks to mathematics consultants:
Debra Harley, Director of Math/Science K–12, East Meadow School District
Allan Brimer, Math Specialist, New Visions School, Freeport School District
Cover Image: © gthompsonphotography/Veer

Triumph Learning® 136 Madison Avenue, 7th Floor, New York, NY 10016

Printed in the United States of America.
15 14 13 12 11

ALL ABOUT YOUR BOOK

COMMON CORE CLINICS MATH will help you with key concepts.

A **Key Words** box introduces new math words. An **Example** shows you how to solve problems in the lesson.

Each lesson has **Guided Practice**. Hints called **THINK** and **REMEMBER** help you work through the problem.

There are two pages of **Independent Practice** with problems for you to solve on your own. You will also solve some **Word Problems**.

At the back of your book, there is a **Glossary** and **Math Tools** that will help you work out problems.

Module 3

Measurement, Data, and Geometry

Common Core State Standards

1 Convert Customary Units

Key Words

capacity
customary units
length
weight

Customary units are standard units of measurement used in the United States.

- **Length** is measured in units such as inches, feet, yards, and miles.
- **Weight** is measured in units such as ounces, pounds, and tons.
- **Capacity** is measured in units such as fluid ounces, quarts, and gallons.

To change larger units to smaller units, multiply.

To change smaller units to larger units, divide.

Example

How many inches are in 8 feet 6 inches?

Think: 1 ft = 12 in.

8 ft 6 in. = ☐ in.

To change feet to inches, multiply.

number of feet	×	number of inches in 1 foot	=	number of inches
↓		↓		↓
8	×	12	=	96

To get the total number of inches, add the 6 inches.

96 + 6 = 102

8 feet 6 inches = 102 inches

APPLY

How would you find how many ounces are in 3 pounds 2 ounces? (1 lb = 16 oz)

Guided Practice

1 To make costumes for the school play, Mrs. Ruiz needs 28 feet of fabric. How many yards of fabric should she buy? Hint: 1 yd = 3 ft

Step 1 Decide if you should multiply or divide.

To change smaller units to larger units,

____________________________________.

> **THINK**
> A foot is smaller than a yard.
> I am changing smaller units to larger units.

Step 2 Write the division sentence. Then divide.

28 ÷ ______ = ______ R1

Step 3 Decide what the remainder means

A remainder of 1 means $\frac{1}{3}$ yard.

Step 4 Add the remainder to the quotient.

______ + $\frac{1}{3}$ = ______

Mrs. Ruiz should buy ______ yards of fabric.

> **THINK**
> The quotient is in yards, so the remainder is in yards, too.
> 3 ft = 1 yd
> 2 ft = $\frac{2}{3}$ yd
> 1 ft = $\frac{1}{3}$ yd

2 Liam made 25 quarts of punch for the school picnic. How many cups of punch did he make? Hint: 1 qt = 4 c

Step 1 Decide if you should multiply or divide.

To change larger units to smaller units,

____________________________________.

> **THINK**
> A quart is larger than a cup.
> I am changing larger units to smaller units.

Step 2 Write the multiplication sentence. Then multiply.

25 × ______ = ______

Liam made ______ cups of punch.

Independent Practice

Use the tables on page 47 to answer the questions on pages 6 and 7.

1. How do you change feet to inches?

____

____

2. How do you change ounces to pounds?

____

____

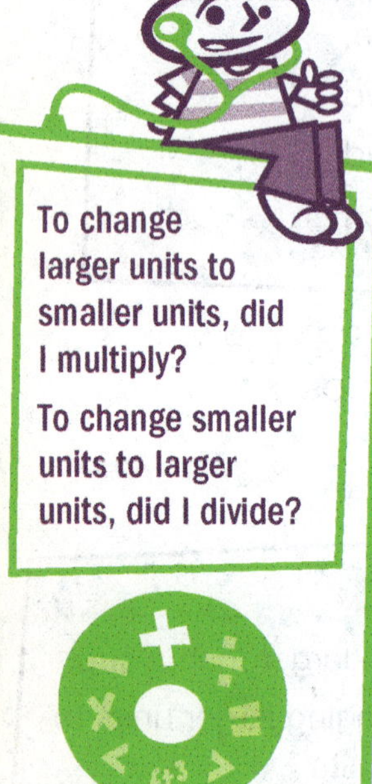

Use what you know about customary units to complete each pattern.

3. 1 ft = 12 in.

2 ft = _____ in.

3 ft = _____ in.

4 ft = _____ in.

5 ft = _____ in.

4. 16 oz = 1 lb

32 oz = _____ lb

48 oz = _____ lb

64 oz = _____ lb

80 oz = _____ lb

5. 1 c = 8 oz

2 c = _____ oz

3 c = _____ oz

4 c = _____ oz

5 c = _____ oz

6 c = _____ oz

6. 3 ft = 1 yd

4 ft = $1\frac{1}{3}$ yd

5 ft = _____ yd

6 ft = _____ yd

7 ft = _____ yd

8 ft = _____ yd

Change the unit.

7. 7 ft = ______ in.
8. 5 gal = ______ qt
9. 4,000 lb = ______ T
10. 36 in. = ______ ft
11. 2 mi = ______ ft
12. 20 ft = ______ yd
13. 72 in. = ______ yd
14. 14 c = ______ qt
15. 100 gal = ______ qt
16. 9,000 lb = ______ T
17. 130 oz = ______ lb
18. 3 yd = ______ in.
19. How many fluid ounces are in $6\frac{1}{2}$ cups? ______
20. How many pounds are in 5 tons? ______
21. How many yards are in 31 ft? ______
22. How many gallons are in 50 qt? ______

Solve each problem.

23. Mr. Johnson bought $9\frac{1}{2}$ gallons of lemonade for the school picnic. How many quarts is that?

______

24. A truck weighs 4,500 pounds. How many tons is that?

______

25. A recipe calls for 1 cup of juice in each fruit smoothie. How many cups of juice do you need to make 3 quarts?

______

2 Convert Metric Units

Key Words

gram
liter
meter
metric units

Metric units are units of measurement based on the metric system.

- A **meter (m)** is about the length of 1 yard.
- A **gram (g)** is about the mass of a paper clip.
- A **liter (L)** is about the capacity of 1 quart.

To change larger units to smaller units, multiply.
To change smaller units to larger units, divide.

Example 1

How many centimeters in 3 meters?

Think: 1 m = 100 cm

3 m = ☐ cm

To change meters to centimeters, multiply.

number of m	×	number of cm in 1 m	=	number of cm
↓		↓		↓
3	×	100	=	300

3 m = 300 cm

Example 2

How many kilograms are in 5,500 grams?

Think: 1,000 g = 1 kg

5,500 g = ☐ kg

To change grams to kilograms, divide.

number of g	÷	number of g in 1 kg	=	number of kg
↓		↓		↓
5,500	÷	1,000	=	5.5

5,500 g = 5.5 kg

DISCUSS

How can you find how many liters are in 2,000 milliliters? (1 L = 1,000 mL)

Guided Practice

1 Ripley has 4.5 liters of water. How many milliliters of water is that?

Step 1 Decide if you should multiply or divide.

To change larger units to smaller units,

__________.

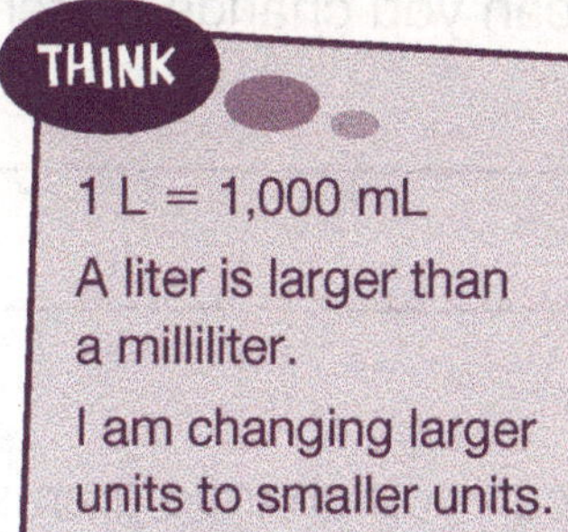

Step 2 Write the multiplication sentence. Then multiply.

4.5 × ______ = ______

Ripley has ______ milliliters of water.

2 The mass of a cat is 6,200 grams. How many kilograms is that?

Step 1 Decide if you should multiply or divide.

To change smaller units to larger units,

__________.

THINK

1,000 g = 1 kg

A gram is smaller than a kilogram.

I am changing smaller units to larger units.

Step 2 Write the division sentence. Then divide.

6,200 ÷ ______ = ______

The cat's mass is ______ kilograms.

Independent Practice

Use the tables on page 48 to answer the questions on pages 10 and 11.

1. How can you change meters to centimeters?

____

____

2. How can you change grams to kilograms?

____

____

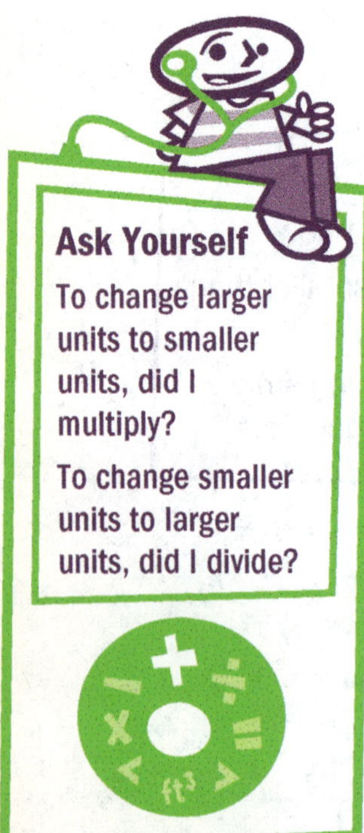

Use what you know about metric units to complete each pattern.

3. 1,000 g = 1 kg

   2,000 g = ________ kg

   3,000 g = ________ kg

   4,000 g = ________ kg

   5,000 g = ________ kg

4. 10 L = 10,000 mL

   20 L = ________ mL

   30 L = ________ mL

   40 L = ________ mL

   50 L = ________ mL

5. 1,500 m = 1.5 km

   2,500 m = ________ km

   3,500 m = ________ km

   4,500 m = ________ km

   5,500 m = ________ km

6. 10 mm = 1 cm

   15 mm = ________ cm

   20 mm = ________ cm

   25 mm = ________ cm

   30 mm = ________ cm

Change the unit.

7. 4,000 mL = _______ L
8. 50 kg = _______ g
9. 2,400 m = _______ km

10. 950 cm = _______ m
11. 100 mm = _______ cm
12. 2 m = _______ mm

13. 253 L = _______ mL
14. 500 g = _______ kg
15. 2.5 L = _______ mL

16. How many millimeters are in 180 centimeters? _________

17. How many grams are 0.3 kilogram? _________

18. How many meters are in 2.7 kilometers? _________

19. How many liters are in 42,000 milliliters? _________

Compare. Write <, >, or =.

20. 1.5 m ◯ 1.5 km
21. 2,000 g ◯ 2 kg
22. 30 mm ◯ 0.3 cm

Solve each problem.

23. Miguel is doing a science experiment. He measures 80 milliliters of water into a beaker. How many liters is that?

____

24. Lori ran a 10-kilometer race. After the race, she jogged for 500 meters to cool down. How many meters did she run in all?

____

3 Understand Volume

Volume is the amount of space enclosed by a solid figure. Volume is measured in **cubic units**. A cubic unit is a cube that is one unit by one unit by one unit. You can find the volume of a solid figure by counting how many cubes will fit in it.

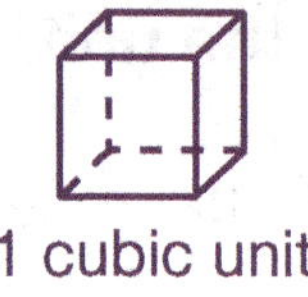

1 cubic unit

Example

What is the volume of the box?

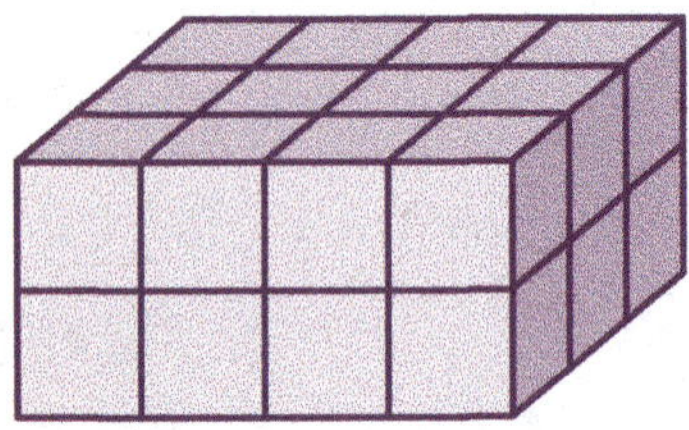

The model shows the length, width, and height of the box.

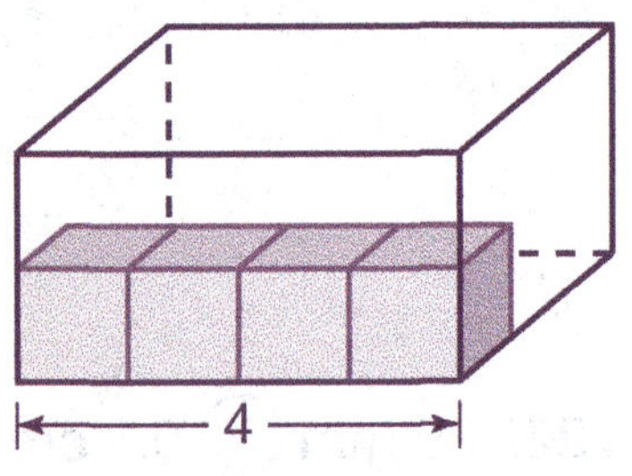

length: 4 cubes

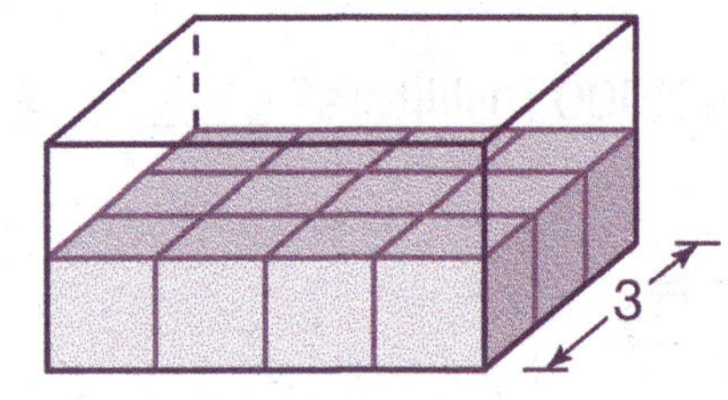

width: 3 cubes

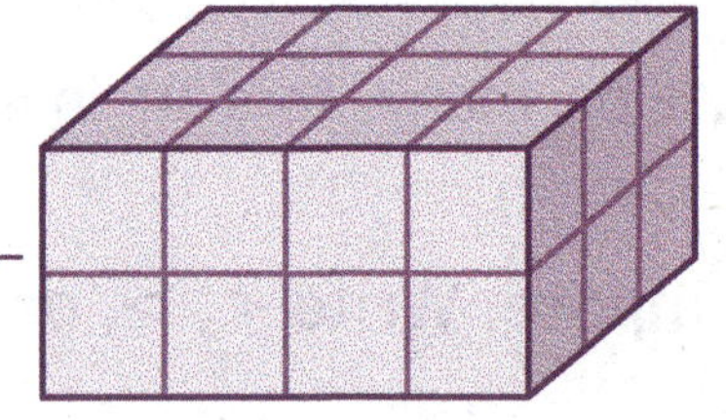

height: 2 cubes

One way to find the volume is to count the cubes.

The bottom layer has 12 cubes.
The top layer has 12 cubes.

Since each layer has the same number of cubes, you can multiply to find the total number of cubic units.

number of layers	×	number of cubes per layer	=	total number of cubes
↓		↓		↓
2	×	12	=	24

The volume of the box is 24 cubic units.

DEMONSTRATE

Use cubes or a drawing to explain how to find the volume of a box that is 2 cubes long, 2 cubes wide, and 2 cubes high.

Guided Practice

What is the volume of the box in cubic inches?

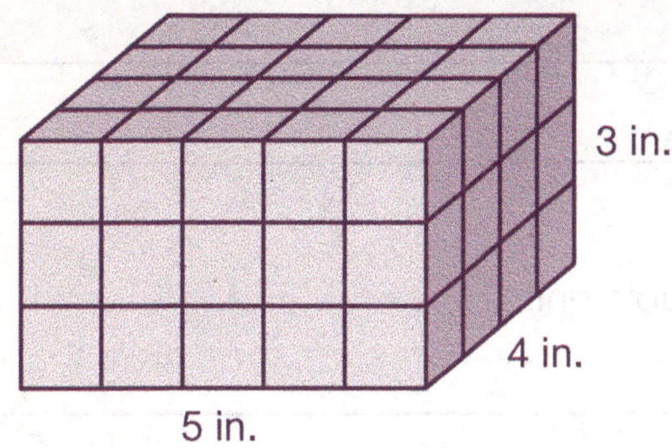

Step 1 Find the number of cubic inches in each layer.

The length of the box is _____ cubic inches.

The width of the box is _____ cubic inches.

There are _____ cubic inches in each layer.

> **THINK**
>
> 1 cube = 1 cubic inch
>
> I can count the cubes to find how many are in a layer.

Step 2 Find the number of layers.

There are _____ layers of cubes.

Step 3 Multiply.

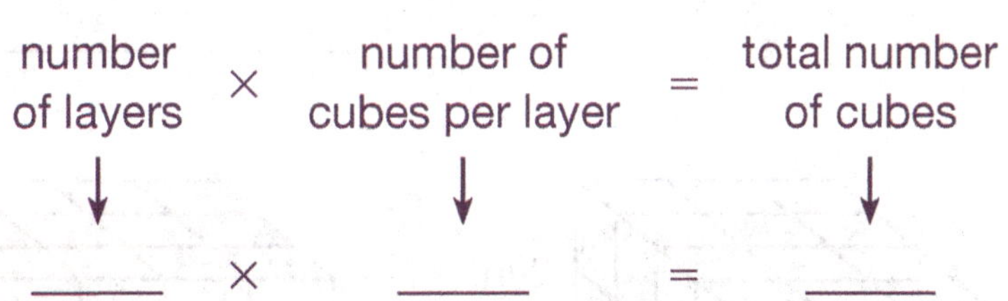

The volume of the box is _____ cubic inches.

Independent Practice

1. How can you use cubes to find the volume of a box?

____

____

2. How can you find the volume of a box in cubic units?

____

____

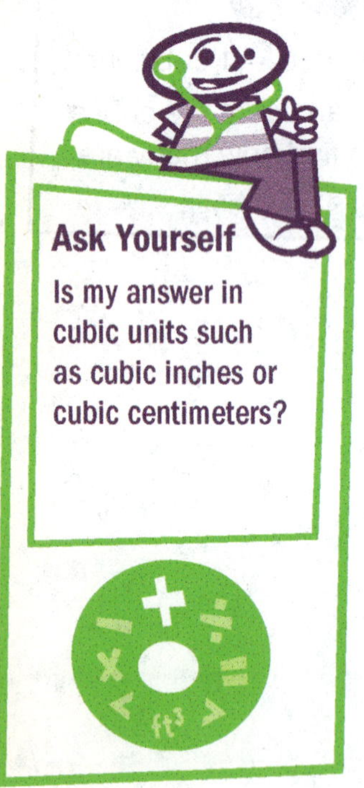

Ask Yourself

Is my answer in cubic units such as cubic inches or cubic centimeters?

Find the volume of each box.

3.

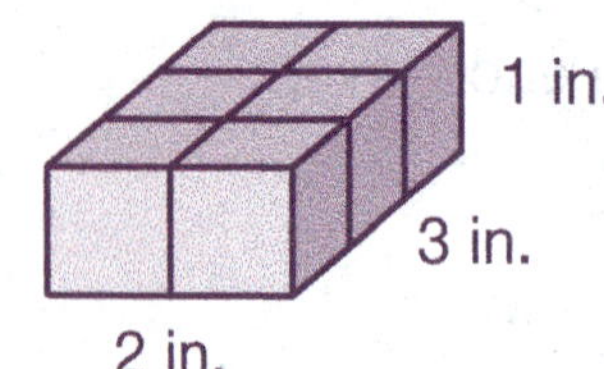

____

4.

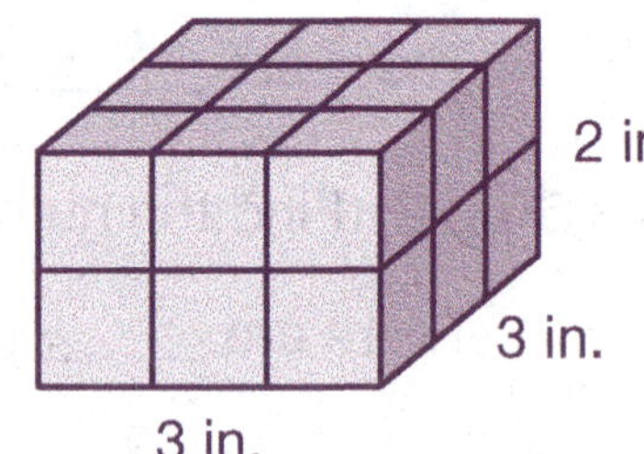

____

5.

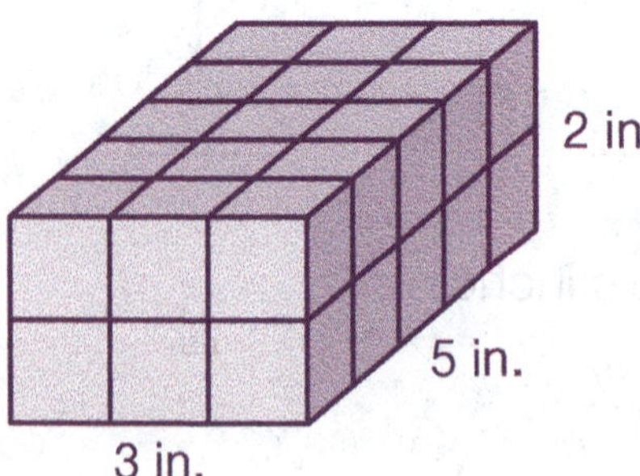

____

6.

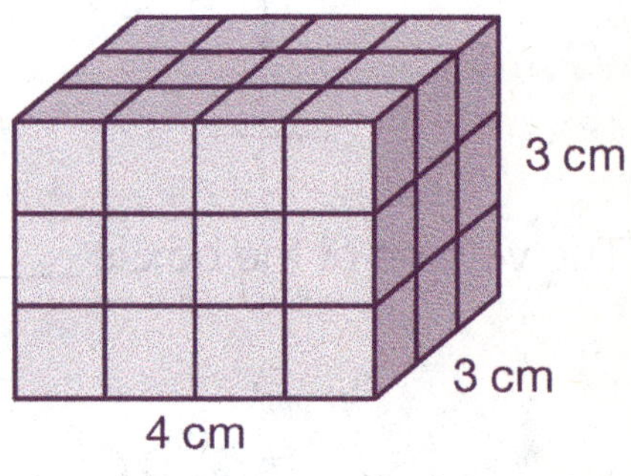

____

Find the volume.

7.

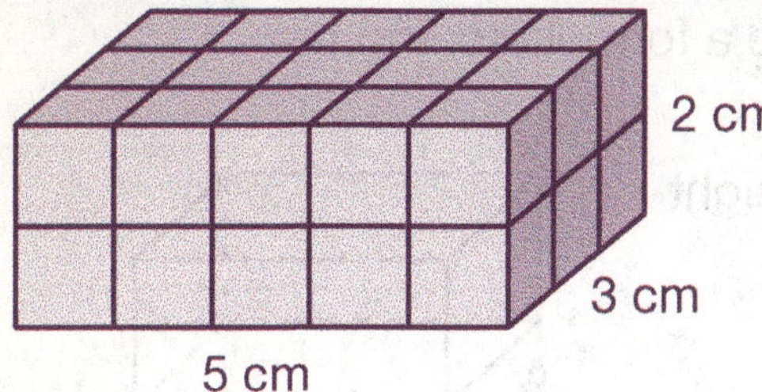

____

8.

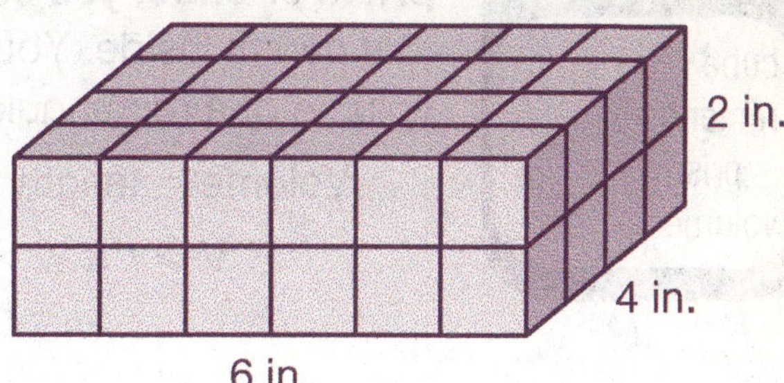

____

9.

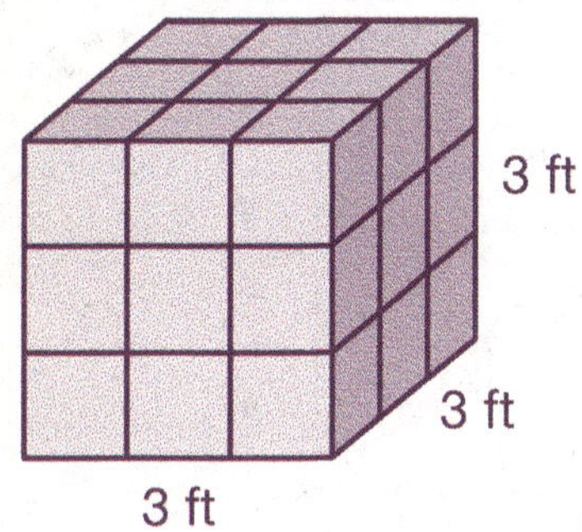

____

10.

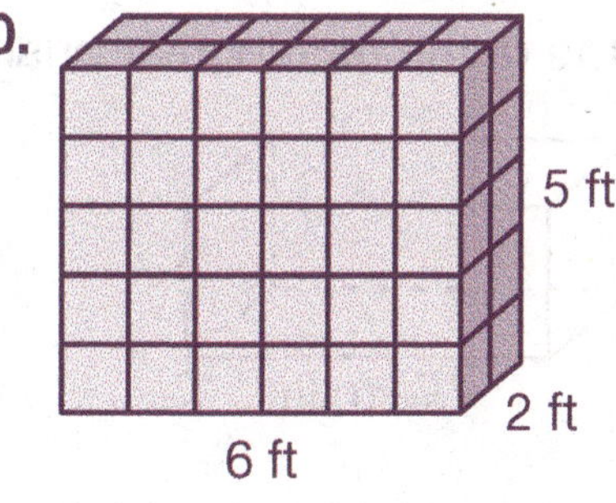

____

Solve each problem.

The drawing shows how Khalil is stacking cubes in a rectangular-shaped storage bin.

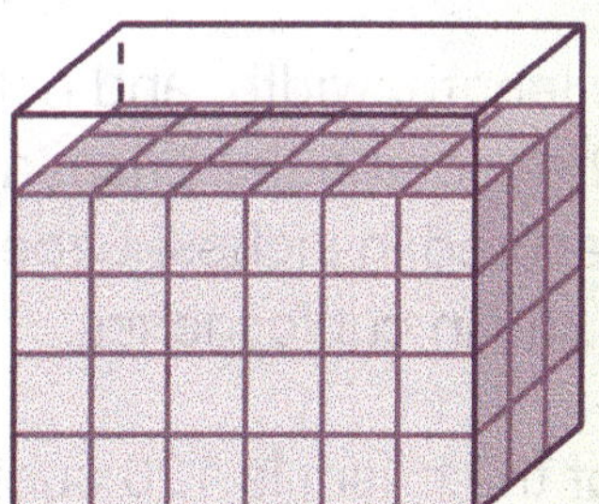

11. How many more cubes can Khalil fit in the storage bin? ______________

12. What is the total number of cubes he can put in the storage bin? ______________

4 Volumes of Rectangular Prisms

Key Words
- cube
- rectangular prism
- volume

In Lesson 3, you saw that to find the **volume** of a **rectangular prism** or **cube**, you could count the number of cubic units that can fit inside. You can also use a formula to find the volume of a rectangular prism:

Volume = length × width × height

$V = l \times w \times h$

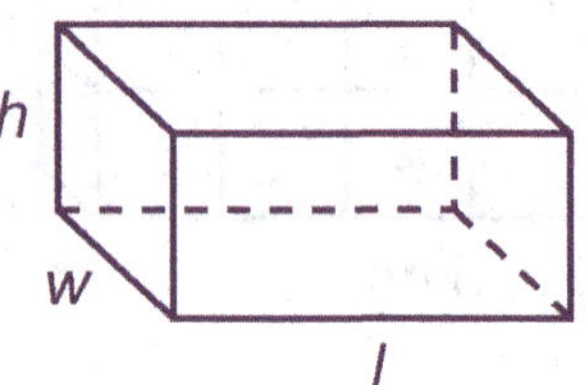

Example

What is the volume of the rectangular prism?

$h = 4$ in.

$w = 3$ in.

$l = 10$ in.

Use the formula. Multiply length times width times height.

Volume $= l \times w \times h$

$V = 10 \times 3 \times 4$

$V = 30 \times 4$

$V = 120$

The length, width, and height of the rectangular prism are measured in inches. Label the volume in cubic inches.

The volume of the prism is 120 cubic inches.

CONCLUDE

Suppose you have cubes that are 1 in. × 1 in. × 1 in. How many 1-inch cubes would fit inside a rectangular prism that has a volume of 60 cubic inches? Explain.

Guided Practice

What is the volume of the cube?

5 in.
5 in.
5 in.

Step 1 Use the formula. Write the cube's length, width, and height.

$V = l \times w \times h$

$V = 5 \times$ ___ $\times$ ___

THINK

The sides of a cube are equal. The length, width, and height of the cube are 5 inches.

Step 2 Find the volume. Multiply.

$V = 5 \times 5 \times 5$

$V = 25 \times 5$

$V =$ ____

Step 3 Determine the label for the volume.

The length, width, and height of the cube are measured in ______________________.

Label the volume in ______________________.

REMEMBER

Volume is always given in cubic units such as cubic inches, cubic feet, or cubic centimeters.

The volume of the cube is ______________________.

Independent Practice

1. How would you find the volume of a cube with sides of 4 inches?

____

____

Ask Yourself

Did I use the volume formula?

Is my answer in cubic units such as cubic inches or cubic centimeters?

Find the volume of each rectangular prism.

2. 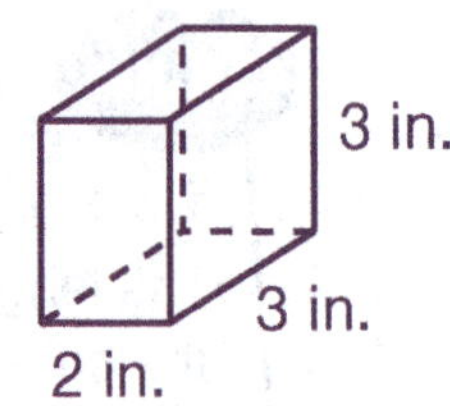

$V = 2 \times 3 \times 3$

$V =$ ____________

3. 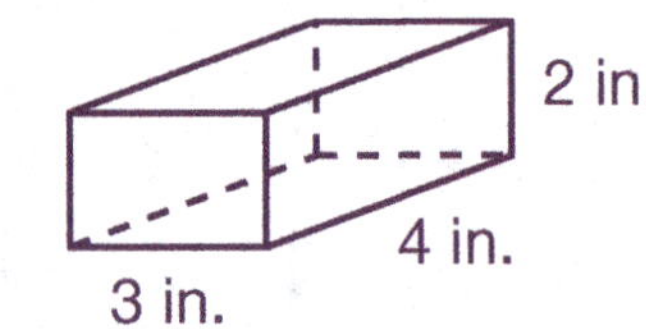

$V = 3 \times 4 \times 2$

$V =$ ____________

4. 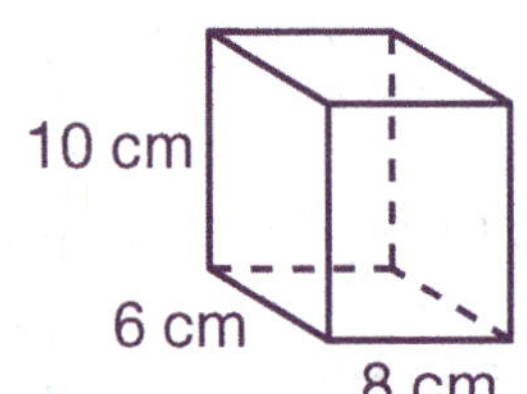

$V =$ _____ × _____ × _____

$V =$ ____________

5. 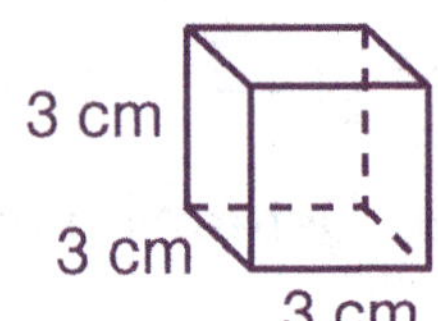

$V =$ _____ × _____ × _____

$V =$ ____________

6. A shipping company sells boxes with the dimensions shown. What is the volume of the box?

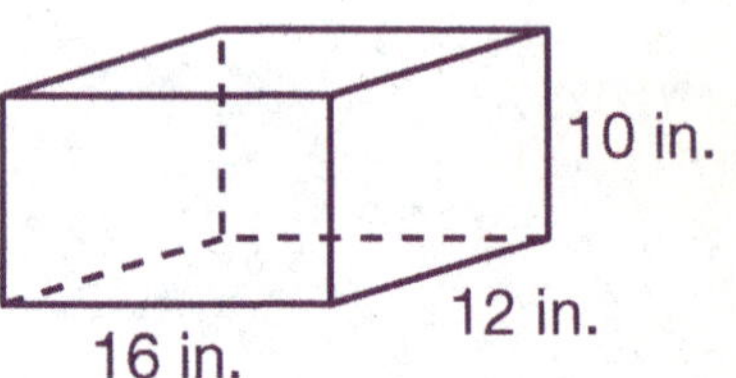

____

Find the volume.

7.

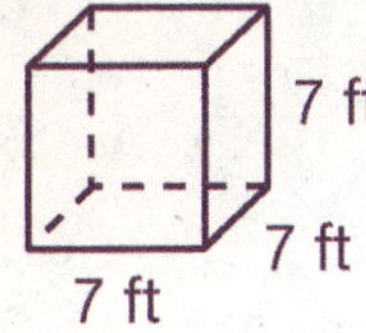

____

8.

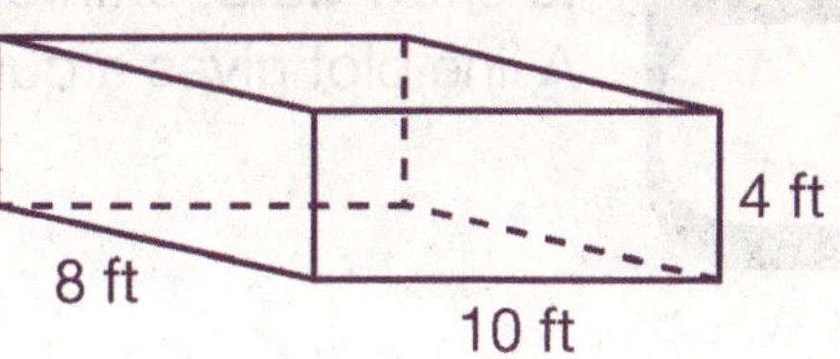

____

9.

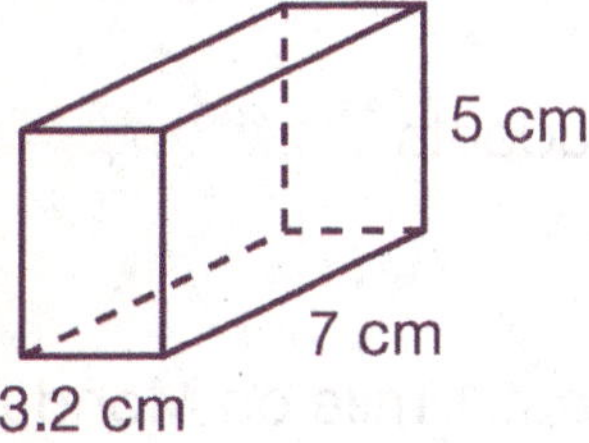

____

10.

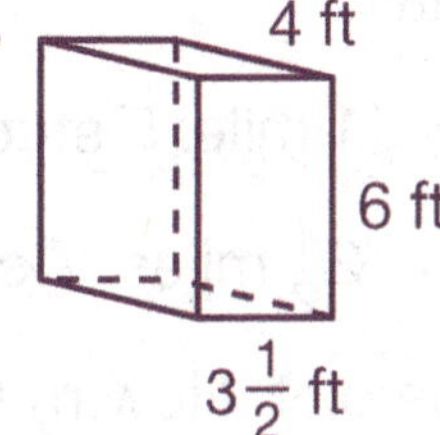

____

Solve each problem.

11. Mali designs packaging. She puts two small boxes together to make one large box.

What is the volume of each small box?

____

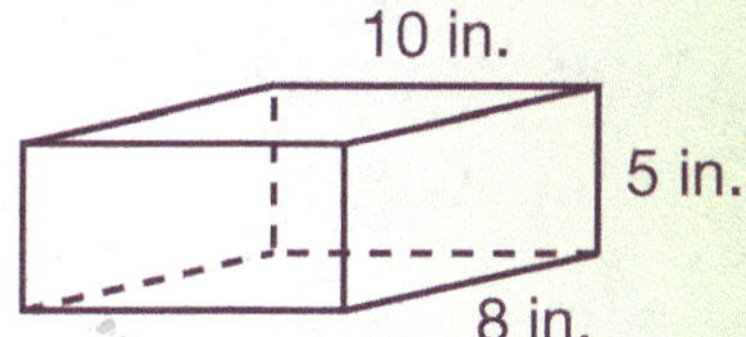

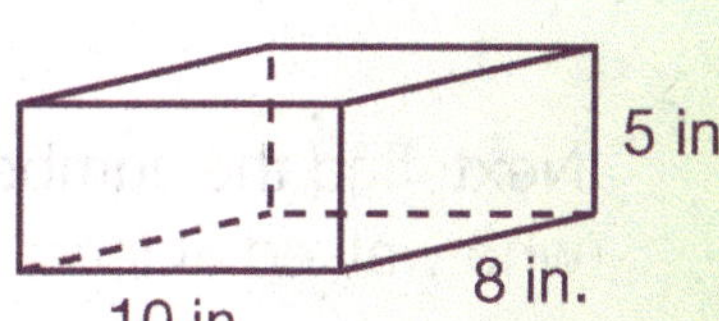

12. The large box Mali makes has these dimensions: $l = 10$ in. $w = 8$ in. $h = 10$ in.

What is its volume?

____

5 Line Plots

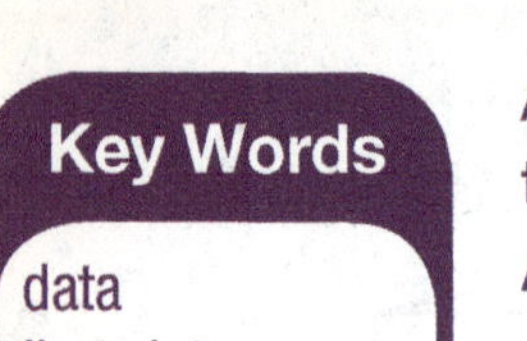

A **line plot** is a graph that uses a number line and Xs or dots to show **data**, or information collected about people or things. A line plot gives a quick picture of data.

Example

The students in Mrs. Tang's gym class are keeping track of their miles walked. This is their data for Monday:

$\frac{1}{2}$ mile: 4 students   1 mile: 5 students $1\frac{1}{2}$ miles: 8 students

2 miles: 0 students $2\frac{1}{2}$ miles: 7 students

Use the data to make a line plot. How many students walked at least 1 mile on Monday?

Make a line plot.

Find the miles walked. Make 1 X for each student who walked that number of miles.

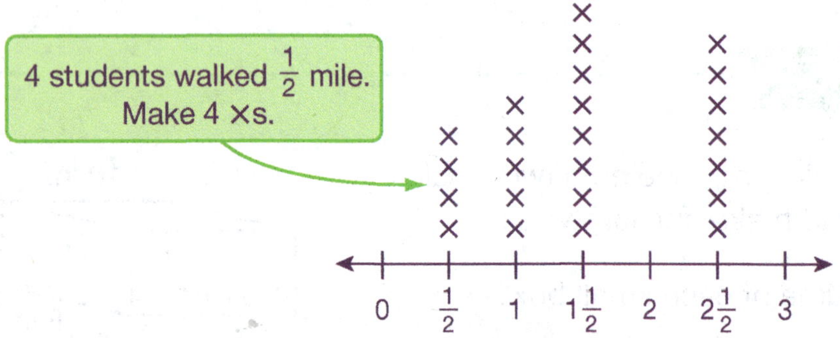

Next, find the number of students who walked at least 1 mile.

"At least" means 1 mile or more. Find the total number of Xs above 1, $1\frac{1}{2}$, 2, $2\frac{1}{2}$, and 3.

There are 5 Xs above 1, 8 Xs above $1\frac{1}{2}$, and 7 Xs above $2\frac{1}{2}$.

$5 + 8 + 7 = 20$

20 students walked at least 1 mile on Monday.

APPLY

Suppose 3 students walked 2 miles. How would you show the data on the line plot?

Guided Practice

Nova tested the amount of salt in packages of salted nuts such as peanuts, mixed nuts, and so on. Here is her data.

0 teaspoon of salt: 0 packages

$\frac{1}{10}$ teaspoon of salt: 5 packages

$\frac{2}{10}$ teaspoon of salt: 3 packages

$\frac{3}{10}$ teaspoon of salt: 1 package

$\frac{4}{10}$ teaspoon of salt: 1 package

Use the data to make a line plot. How many packages contain less than $\frac{3}{10}$ teaspoon of salt?

Step 1 Complete the line plot. Make Xs above the correct fraction of a teaspoon.

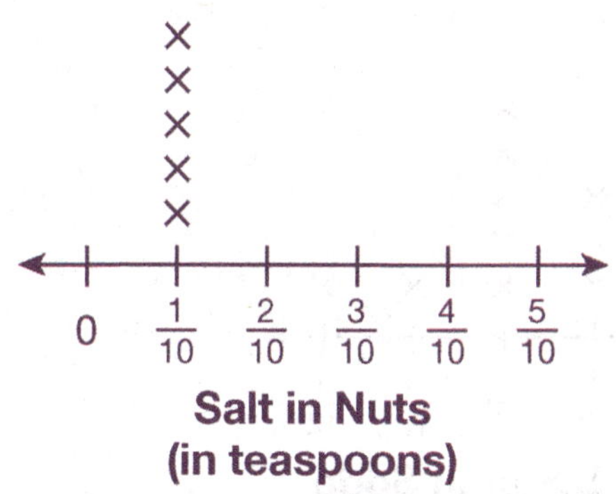

THINK

3 packages of nuts had $\frac{2}{10}$ teaspoon of salt. I should make 3 Xs above $\frac{2}{10}$.

Step 2 Next, find the number of packages that contain less than $\frac{3}{10}$ teaspoon of salt.

There are _____ Xs above $\frac{1}{10}$.

There are _____ Xs above $\frac{2}{10}$.

Add: _____ + _____ = _____

_____ packages contain less than $\frac{3}{10}$ teaspoon of salt.

THINK

The question asks about packages that contain *less than* $\frac{3}{10}$ teaspoon of salt, so don't count the packages that contain $\frac{3}{10}$ teaspoon of salt.

Independent Practice

1. What do the Xs on a line plot show?

___

___

2. Compare the line plots on pages 20 and 21. How can you tell which piece of data occurred most often? Least often?

___

___

For questions 3–6, use the line plot.

Drew tested the amount of sugar in 10 sodas. The line plot shows his data.

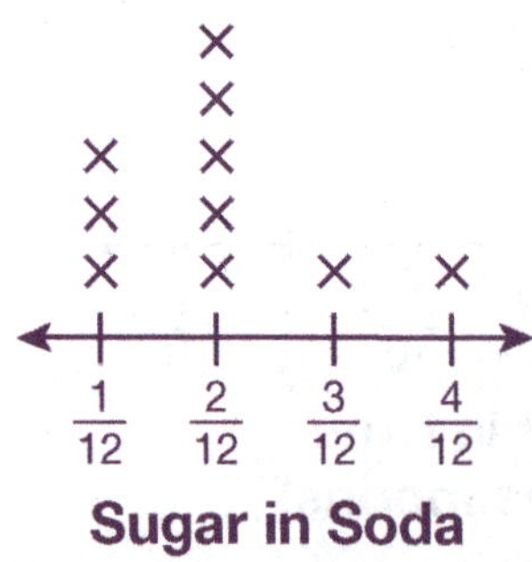

Sugar in Soda (in cups)

3. Which amount(s) occurs most often? ___

4. Which amount(s) occur least often? ___

5. How many sodas that Drew tested contain more than $\frac{2}{12}$ cups of sugar?

___

For questions 6–11, use the data in the table.

For two weeks, Artie kept track of how long he walked his dog each day.

Time Spent Walking the Dog

Amount of Time (in hours)	Number of Days
0	1
$\frac{1}{4}$	3
$\frac{1}{2}$	4
$\frac{3}{4}$	2
1	4

6. Complete the line plot to show Artie's data.

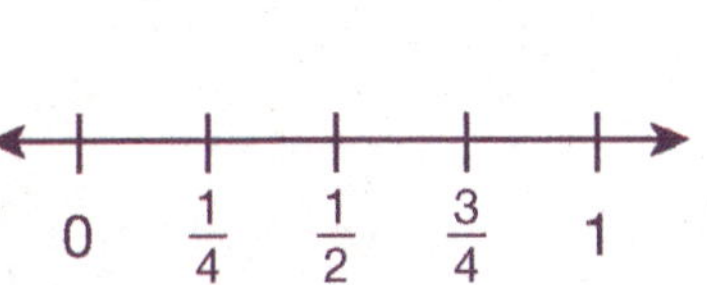

Time Spent Walking the Dog (in hours)

7. Which amount(s) occur most often? ________________

8. Which amount(s) occur least often? ________________

9. How many days did Artie walk the dog for less than $\frac{1}{2}$ hour?

____

10. How many days did Artie walk the dog for 1 hour?

____

11. How many days did Artie walk the dog at least $\frac{1}{2}$ hour?

____

6 Coordinate System

Key Words

coordinate plane
ordered pair
origin
x-axis
x-coordinate
y-axis
y-coordinate

An **ordered pair** (*x*, *y*) is a pair of numbers used to locate a point on a coordinate plane. A **coordinate plane** is formed by the intersection of the ***x*-axis** and ***y*-axis**. The point where the axes meet is called the **origin** and is named by the ordered pair (0, 0).

The first number of an ordered pair is the ***x*-coordinate**. It tells how many horizontal spaces the point is from the origin. The second number of the ordered pair is the ***y*-coordinate**. It tells how many vertical spaces the point is from the origin. On the coordinate plane, point *A* is at (2, 6). The *x*-coordinate is 2. The *y*-coordinate is 6.

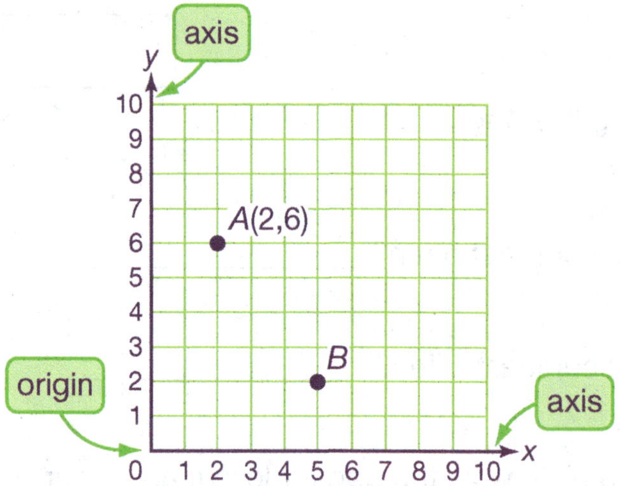

Example

The *x*-coordinate of point *B* is 5. What is its *y*-coordinate?

Use the *y*-axis to find the *y*-coordinate.

Put your finger on point *B*. Move left in a straight line until you touch the *y*-axis. Read the number on the *y*-axis that is directly left of point *B*. This is the *y*-coordinate, 2.

The *y*-coordinate of point *B* is 2.

APPLY

How could you use the *x*-axis to find the *x*-coordinate of point *B*?

Guided Practice

Look at the coordinate plane. Which ordered pair names point *S*?

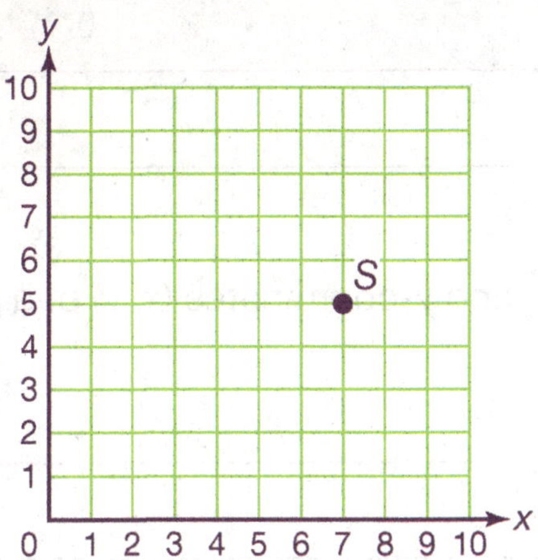

Step 1 Find the *x*-coordinate.

Put your finger on point *S*. Move your finger straight down to the *x*-axis.

The *x*-coordinate is _____.

Step 2 Find the *y*-coordinate.

Put your finger on point *S* again. Move your finger straight left to the *y*-axis.

The *y*-coordinate is _____.

THINK

In an ordered pair (*x*, *y*), the *x*-coordinate is always the first number.

The *y*-coordinate is always the second number.

Point *S* is named by the ordered pair (_____, _____).

Independent Practice

1. What is a coordinate plane?

____

____

2. How can you use the *x*- and *y*-axes to find the *x*- and *y*-coordinates (*x*, *y*) of a point on a coordinate plane?

____

____

Use the coordinate plane for questions 3–6.

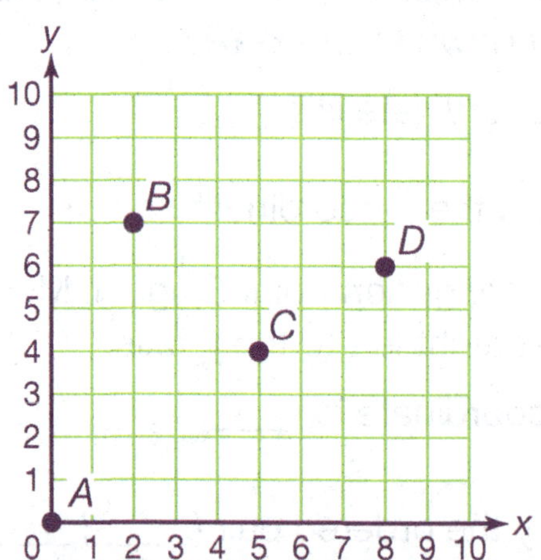

3. Which point is at the origin (0, 0)? _____

4. What is the *x*-coordinate of point *B*? _____

5. What is the *y*-coordinate of point *C*? _____

6. Which ordered pair names point *D*? _______

Use the coordinate plane for questions 7–15.

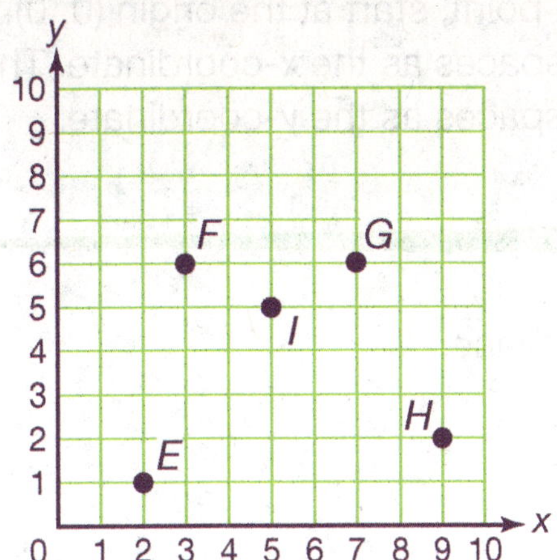

7. What is the x-coordinate of point E? _____

8. What is the y-coordinate of point F? _____

9. Which ordered pair names point E? _______

10. Which ordered pair names point F? _______

11. Which point is named by the ordered pair (5, 5)? _____

12. Which ordered pair names point G? _______

13. How many units above the origin is point H? _____

14. Which ordered pair names point H? _______

15. Taylor says two of the points on the coordinate plane have the same y-coordinate. Which two points are they?

____

7 Ordered Pairs

You can graph an ordered pair (x, y) as a point on a coordinate plane. To graph a point, start at the origin (0, 0). Move right the same number of spaces as the x-coordinate. Then move up the same number of spaces as the y-coordinate.

Example 1

Graph (5, 3) on the coordinate plane.

Start at (0, 0).
Move 5 units to the right.
Move 3 units up.
Draw a point at (5, 3).

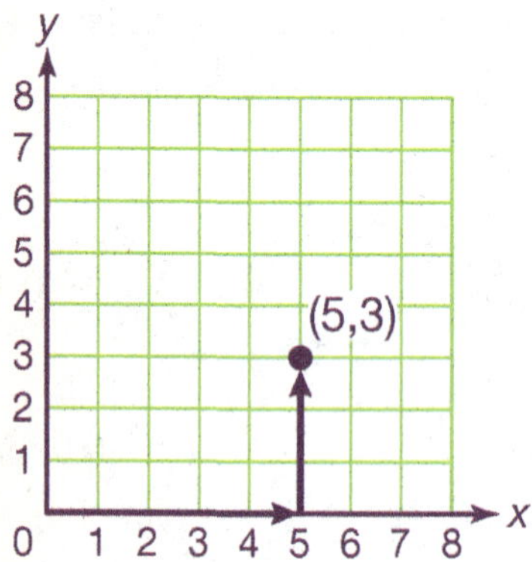

Example 2

Graph (0, 4) on the coordinate plane.

Start at (0, 0).
The x-coordinate is 0. Don't move to the right.
Move 4 units up.
Draw a point at (0, 4).

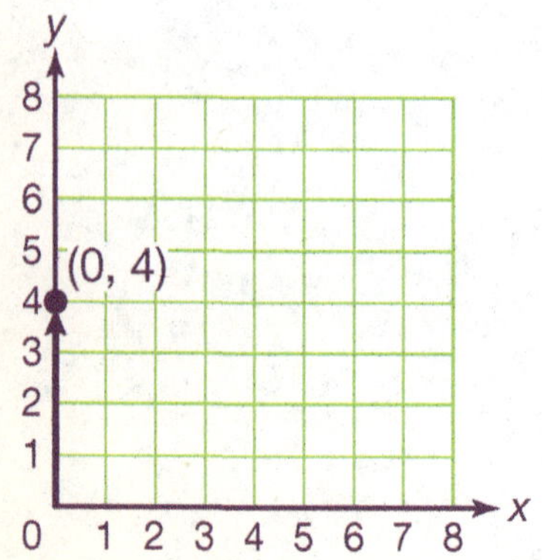

DISCUSS

How would you graph the ordered pair (2, 6) on a coordinate plane?

Guided Practice

1 Graph and label (3, 5) on the coordinate plane.

Step 1 Start at (0, 0).

Step 2 Move 3 units to the right.

Step 3 Move 5 units up.

Step 4 Draw and label a point at (3, 5).

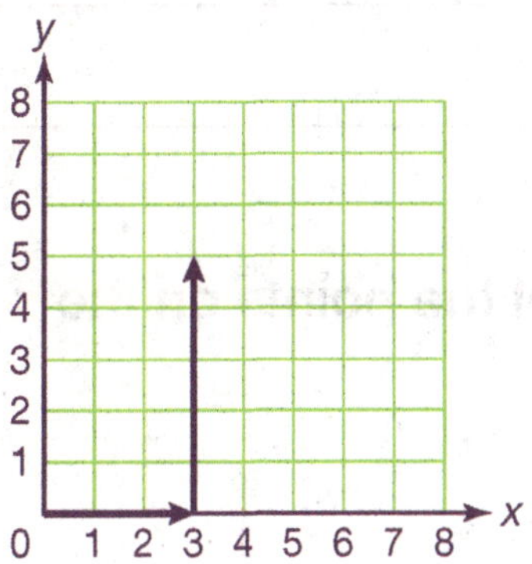

> **REMEMBER**
> The *x*-coordinate shows how far the point is from the origin on the *x*-axis.

> **REMEMBER**
> The *y*-coordinate shows how far the point is from the origin on the *y*-axis.

2 Graph and label (5, 0) on the coordinate plane.

Step 1 Start at (0, 0).

Step 2 Move _____ units to the right.

Step 3 The *y*-coordinate is _____.

Move _____ units up.

Step 4 Draw and label a point at (5, 0).

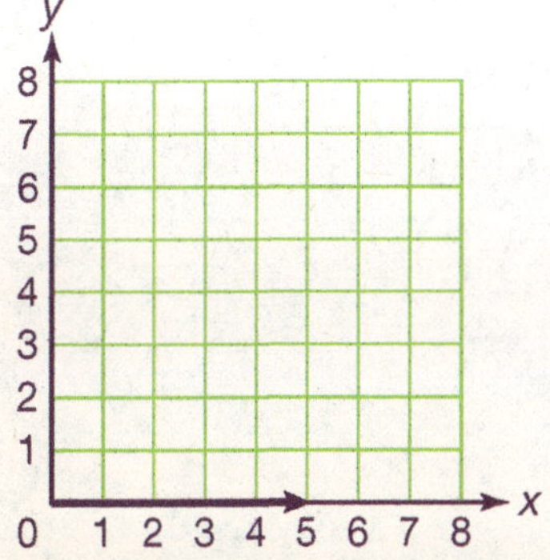

Independent Practice

1. How do you graph a point on a coordinate plane?

____

____

2. Why should you always start at the origin (0, 0) when graphing a point?

____

____

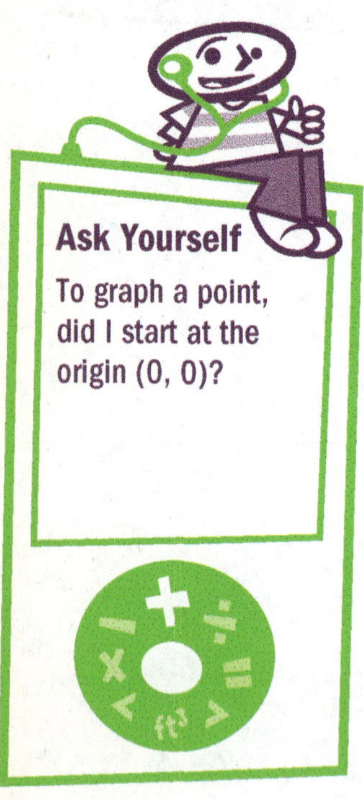

For questions 3–6, graph and label the points on the coordinate plane.

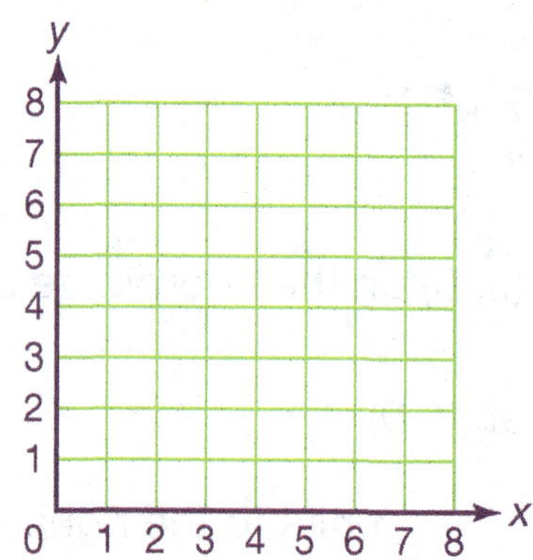

3. *A* (2, 6) 4. *B* (4, 0) 5. *C* (7, 4) 6. *D* (8, 7)

7. Which point is 4 units from the origin (0, 0) on the *x*-axis?

____

For questions 8–15, graph and label the points on the coordinate plane.

8. *E* (1, 8)
9. *F* (2, 6)
10. *G* (4, 8)
11. *H* (5, 5)
12. *I* (7, 3)
13. *J* (7, 1)
14. *K* (8, 7)
15. *L* (9, 4)

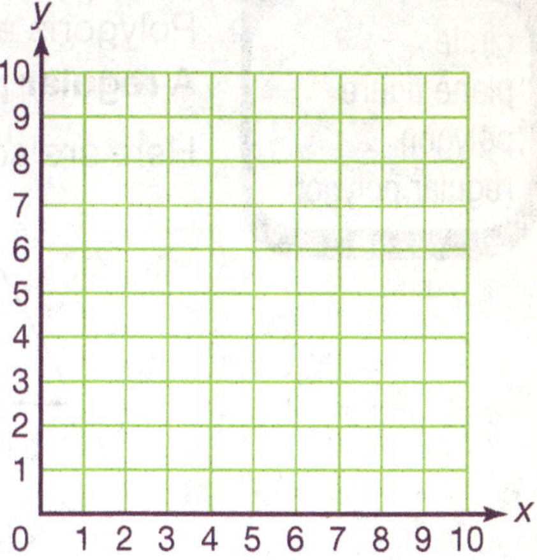

For questions 16–21, name the ordered pair for each point.

16. *M* ______
17. *N* ______
18. *O* ______
19. *P* ______
20. *Q* ______
21. *R* ______

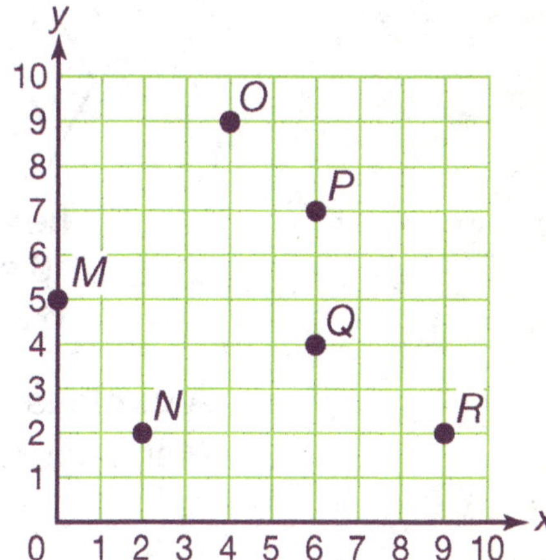

Solve each problem.

Use the map grid for questions 22–23.

22. Which ordered pair gives the location of the school?

____

23. Whose house is at the location (4, 1)?

____

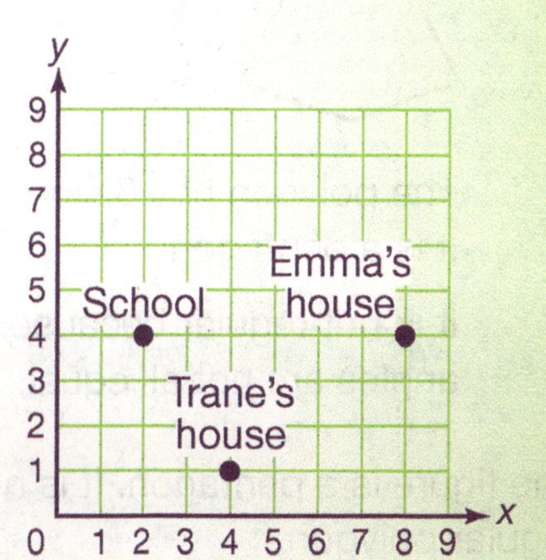

8 Plane Figures

Key Words

circle
plane figure
polygon
regular polygon

A **plane figure** is a flat, two-dimensional figure. A **polygon** is a closed plane figure formed by three or more straight sides. Polygons are named by the number of their sides and angles. A **regular polygon** has all equal sides and all equal angles.

Here are some polygons.

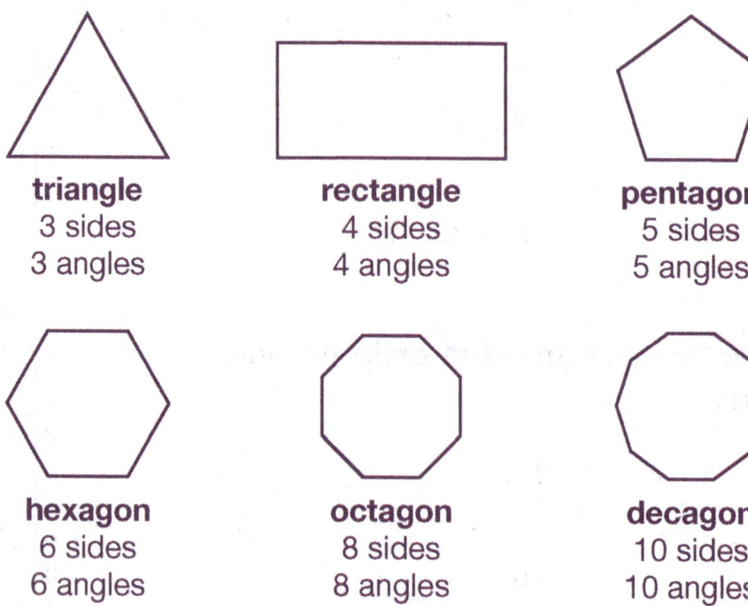

A **circle** is a plane figure that does not have straight sides. Plane figures that do not have straight sides are not polygons.

Example

What is the name of the polygon? Is it a regular polygon?

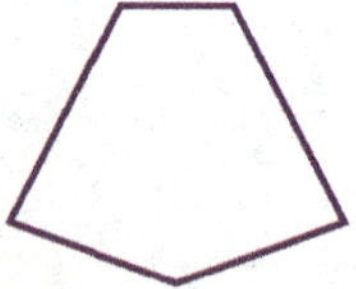

The polygon has 5 sides and 5 angles. It is a pentagon.

It is not regular because its sides and angles are not all equal.

The figure is a pentagon. It is not a regular polygon.

DRAW

Draw a square. Is a square a regular polygon? Explain.

Guided Practice

1 What is the name of the polygon? Is it a regular polygon?

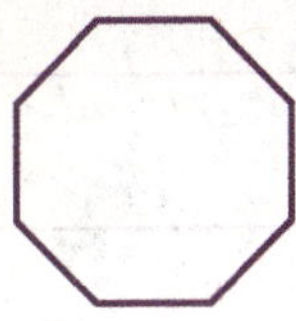

Step 1 Count the sides and angles.

The polygon has _______ sides and _______ angles.

It is a(n) _______________.

Step 2 Compare the sides.

The sides are all the same length.

It **is/is not** a regular polygon.

> **THINK**
> A polygon is regular if all its sides are the same length.

The polygon is a(n) _______________.

It _______________ a regular polygon.

2 Is the figure a circle?

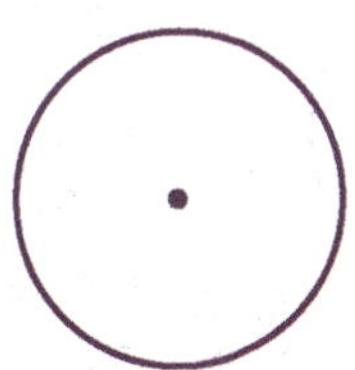

Step 1 Read the definition of a circle. Compare it to the figure.

It is a plane figure that **is/is not** a polygon.

Step 2 Test that the rest of the definition fits.

Every point on the figure **is/is not** the same distance from the center.

> **REMEMBER**
> A circle is a plane figure that is not a polygon because it does not have straight sides. It is a closed figure with all points an equal distance from a point called the center.

The figure is a _______________.

Independent Practice

1. How can you use a polygon's sides or angles to name it?

____

____

2. Explain how to decide if a polygon is regular or not.

____

____

Name each figure.

3. 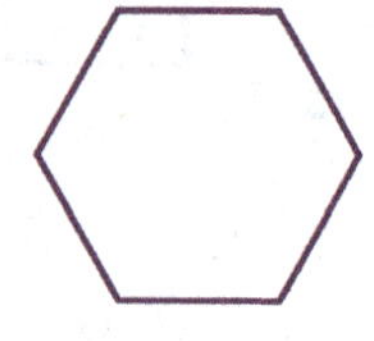

____

4. 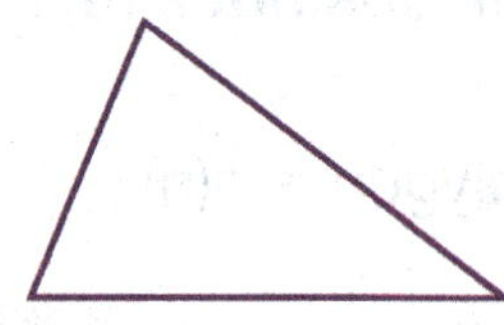

____

5. 

____

6. 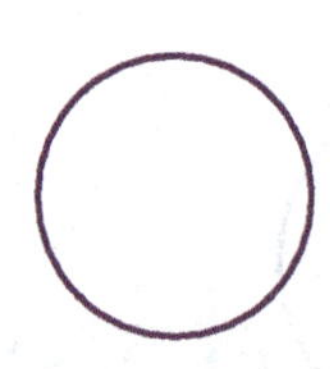

____

7. What kind of polygon is a stop sign?

____

Is it a regular polygon? _______________

Name each polygon. Tell if it is *regular* or *not regular*.

8. 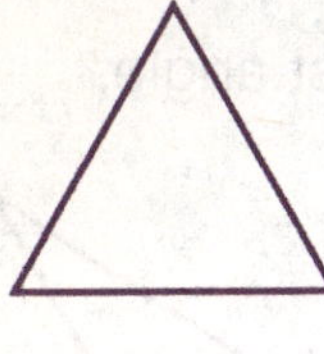

____

9. 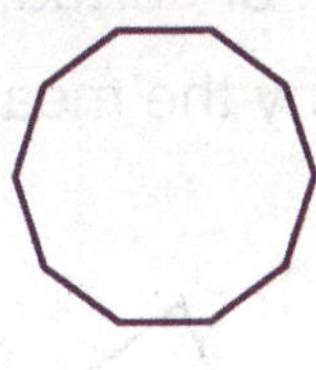

____

10. 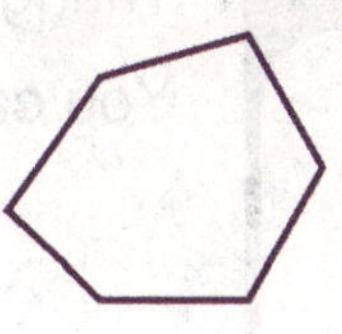

____

11. 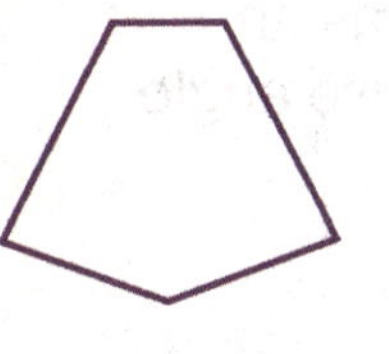

____

12. 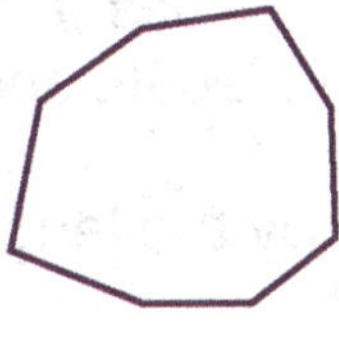

____

13. 

____

14. 

____

15. 

____

16. 

____

Name the figure.

17. I have 5 sides and 5 angles. I am a ________________.

18. I am a closed plane figure. I do not have straight sides. I am a ________________.

19. I have 10 sides and 10 angles. I am a ________________.

9 Triangles

Key Words

acute triangle
equilateral triangle
isosceles triangle
obtuse triangle
right triangle
scalene triangle
triangle

A **triangle** is a polygon with three sides and three angles. Triangles can be classified, or sorted, into groups.

You can classify triangles by the measure of their greatest angle.

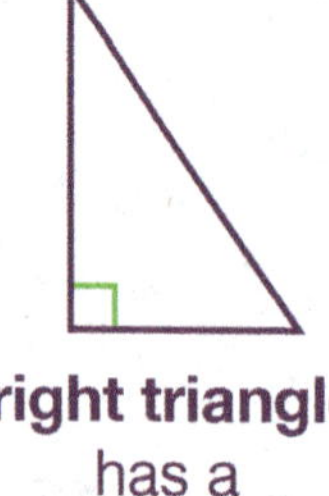

right triangle
has a right angle

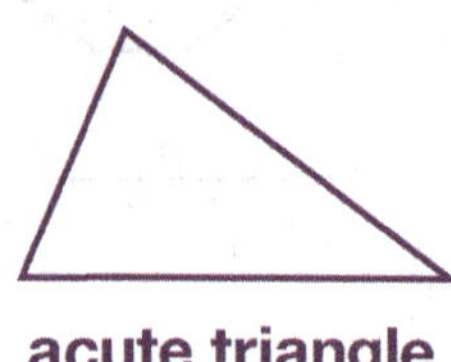

acute triangle
has three acute angles

obtuse triangle
has an obtuse angle

You can classify triangles by the lengths of their sides.

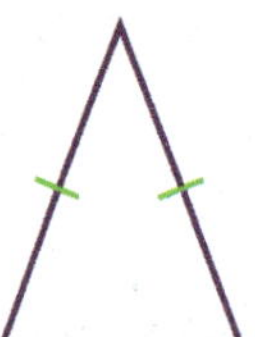

isosceles triangle
At least two sides have equal lengths.

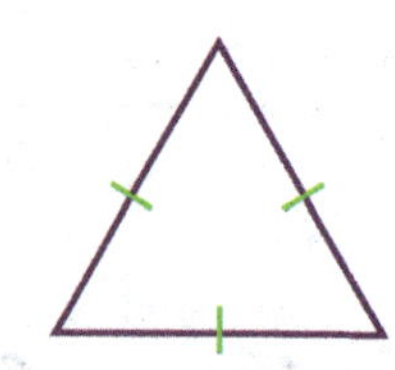

equilateral triangle
All sides have equal lengths.

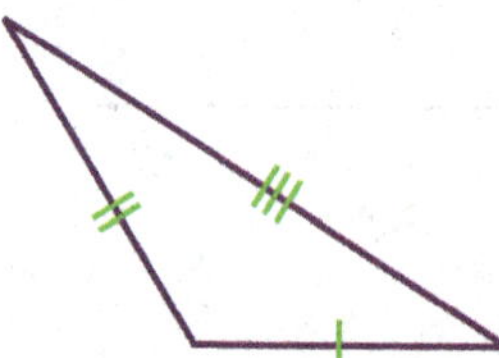

scalene triangle
Each side has a different length.

Example

Classify the triangle by the measure of its angles. Write *right*, *acute*, or *obtuse*.

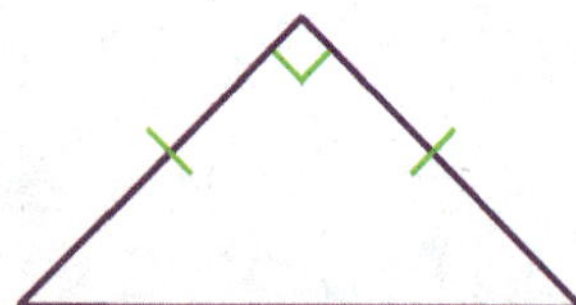

The triangle has a right angle.
It is a *right triangle*.

Classify the same triangle by the lengths of its sides. Write *isosceles*, *equilateral*, or *scalene*.

The triangle has 2 equal sides.
It is an *isosceles triangle*.

The triangle is a right triangle. It is also an isosceles triangle.

DESCRIBE

Look at the other two angles of the right triangles on this page. Are they right, acute, or obtuse angles? What can you say about the angles of a right triangle?

Guided Practice

1 Classify the triangle by the measure of its angles. Write *right*, *acute*, or *obtuse*.

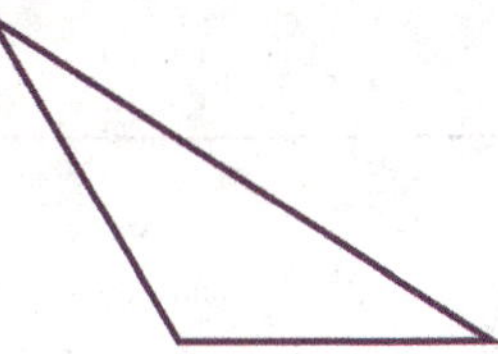

Step 1 Identify the greatest angle measure.

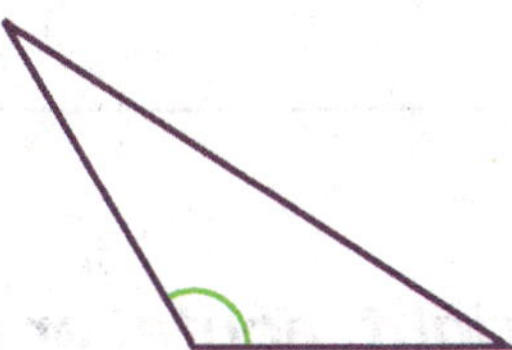

The greatest angle measure is __________ than 90°.

The angle is ______________.

Step 2 Classify the triangle.

The triangle has an obtuse angle.

It is an ______________ triangle.

The triangle is an ______________ triangle.

THINK

Each corner of a paper is a right angle (90°). To decide if an angle is obtuse, line up one edge of the paper with the angle. If the angle is wider than the corner of the paper, it is greater than 90°.

2 Classify the triangle by the lengths of its sides. Write *isosceles*, *equilateral*, or *scalene*.

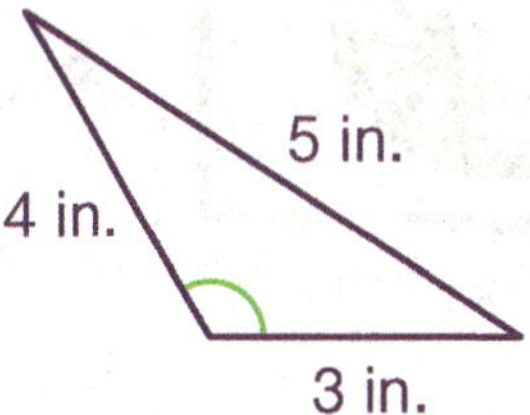

Step 1 Identify the lengths of the sides.

Each side has a different length.

Step 2 Classify the triangle.

It is a ______________ triangle.

The triangle is a ______________ triangle.

THINK

One side is 3 inches long. One side is 4 inches long. One side is 5 inches long. None of the sides have the same length.

Independent Practice

1. How do you classify a triangle by its angles?

____

____

2. How do you classify a triangle by its sides?

____

____

Ask Yourself

Is the angle less than, equal to, or greater than 90°?

How many sides are the same length?

Classify each triangle. Write *right*, *acute*, or *obtuse*.

3. 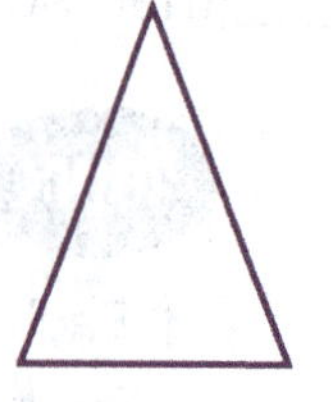

____

4. 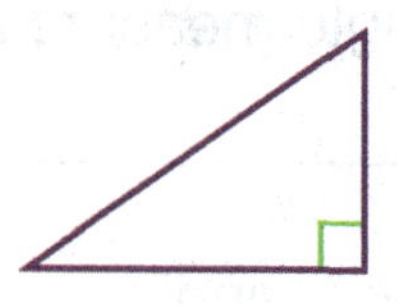

____

5. 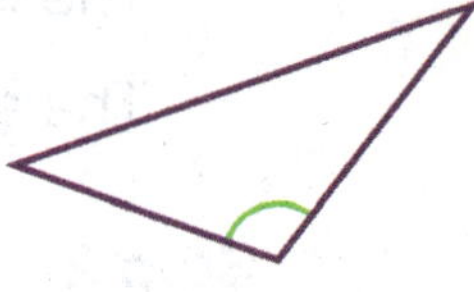

____

Classify each triangle. Write *isosceles*, *equilateral*, or *scalene*.

6. 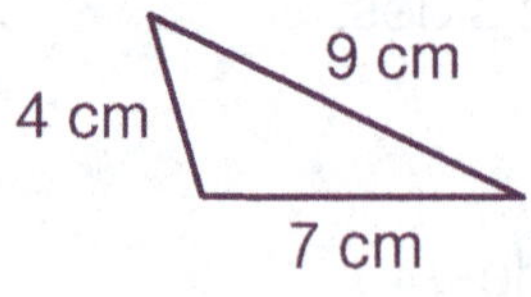

____

7. 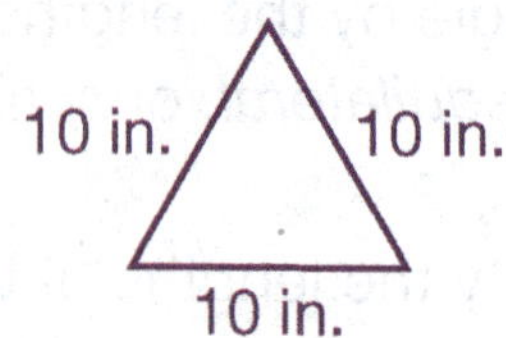

____

8. 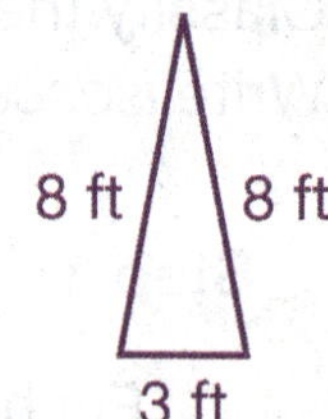

____

9. Is a yield sign in the shape of an isosceles, equilateral, or scalene triangle?

____

Classify each triangle. Write *right*, *acute*, or *obtuse*.

10. 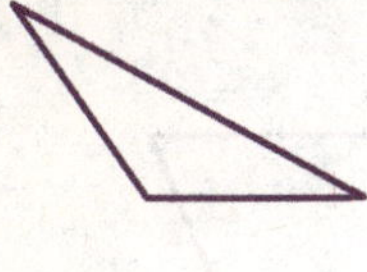

____

11. 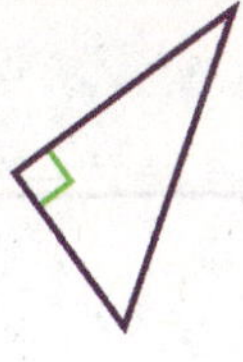

____

12. 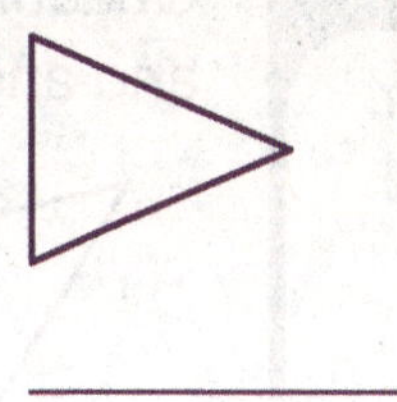

____

Classify each triangle. Write *isosceles*, *equilateral*, or *scalene*.

13. 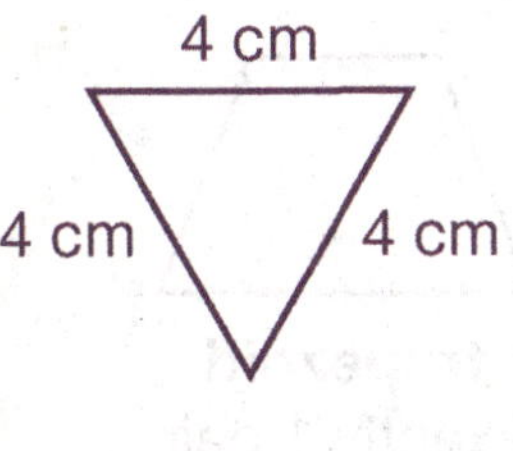

____

14. 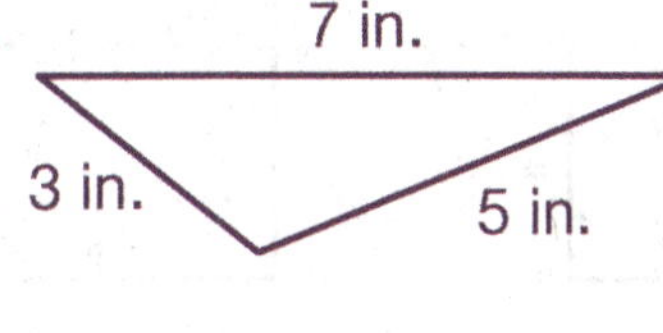

____

15. 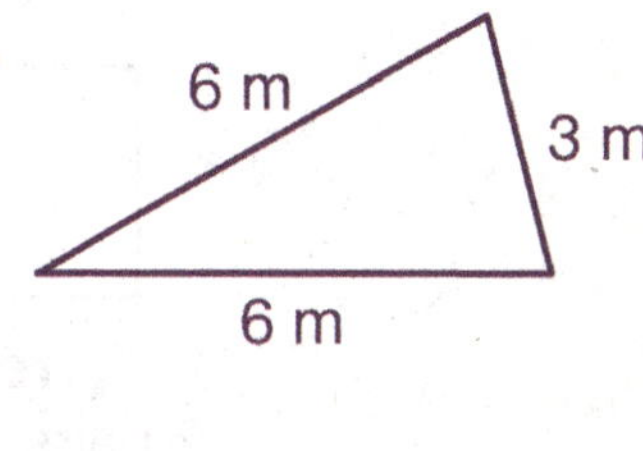

____

Name the triangle.

16. I have three acute angles. I am a(n) ______________ triangle.

17. Each of my sides has a different length. I am a(n) ______________ triangle.

18. I have one obtuse angle. I am a(n) ______________ triangle.

19. I have two sides that are equal. I am a(n) ______________ triangle.

20. Each of my sides are 2 yards long. I am a(n) ______________ triangle.

10 Quadrilaterals

Key Words

parallelogram
quadrilateral
rectangle
rhombus
square
trapezoid

A **quadrilateral** is a polygon with four sides and four angles. Quadrilaterals can be sorted into groups based on their sides and angles.

quadrilateral
4 sides
4 angles

parallelogram
2 pairs of equal sides
2 pairs of parallel sides

rhombus
4 equal sides
2 pairs of parallel sides

rectangle
2 pairs of equal sides
4 right angles

square
4 equal sides
4 right angles

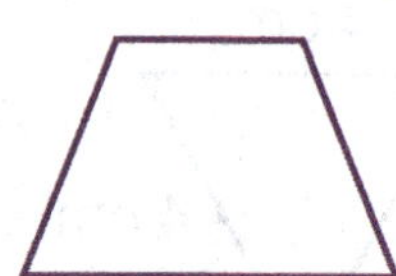

trapezoid
exactly 1 pair of parallel sides

Some quadrilaterals belong to more than one group. For example, a square is a rectangle with four equal sides.

Example

What other groups does a rectangle fit into?

A rectangle has 4 sides and 4 angles, so it is a quadrilateral.

A rectangle has 2 pairs of equal sides and 2 pairs of parallel sides, so it is a parallelogram.

A rectangle can be classified as a quadrilateral and a parallelogram.

COMPARE

How are a square and a rectangle alike? How are they different?

Guided Practice

Classify the figure in as many ways as possible. Write *quadrilateral*, *parallelogram*, *rhombus*, *rectangle*, *square*, or *trapezoid*.

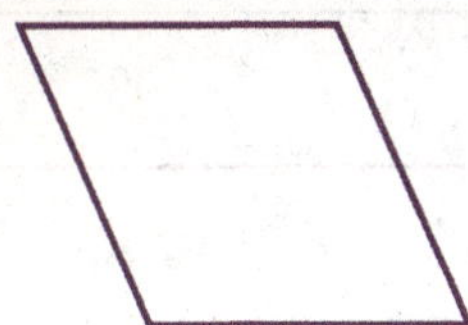

Step 1 Identify the number of sides.

There are 4 sides, so it is a ________________.

Step 2 Identify any pairs of opposite sides that are parallel.

There are 2 pairs of parallel sides, so it is a ________________.

Step 3 Identify any sides that are equal, or have the same length.

All the sides have the same length, so it is a rhombus or a ________________.

Step 4 Identify any right angles.

There are no right angles, so it is **not** a ________________ or a square.

The figure is a ________________, ________________, and a ________________.

THINK

Any polygon with 4 sides is a quadrilateral.

REMEMBER

Two lines are parallel if they never intersect and are the same distance apart at every point.

Independent Practice

1. How can you tell if a polygon is a quadrilateral?

____

____

2. How can you tell if a quadrilateral is a rectangle or a square?

____

____

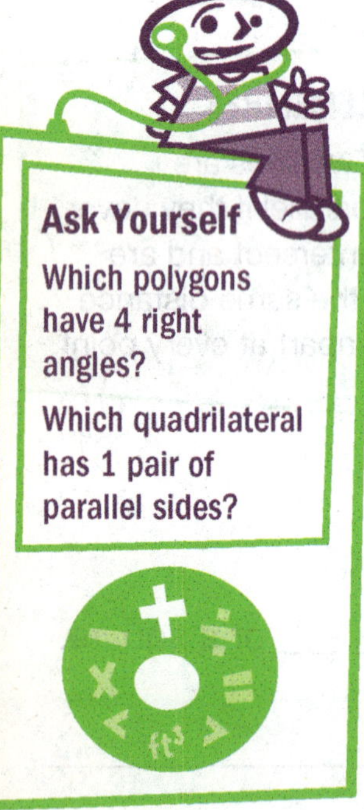

Ask Yourself

Which polygons have 4 right angles?

Which quadrilateral has 1 pair of parallel sides?

Classify the figure in as many ways as possible. Write *quadrilateral*, *parallelogram*, *rhombus*, *rectangle*, *square*, or *trapezoid*.

3. 

____

____

4. 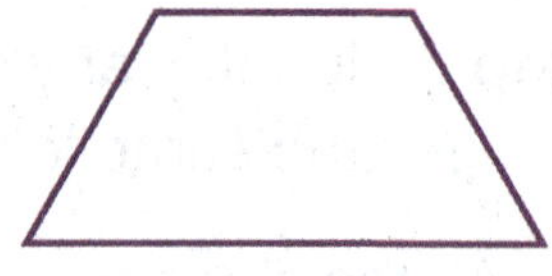

____

____

5. 

____

____

6. 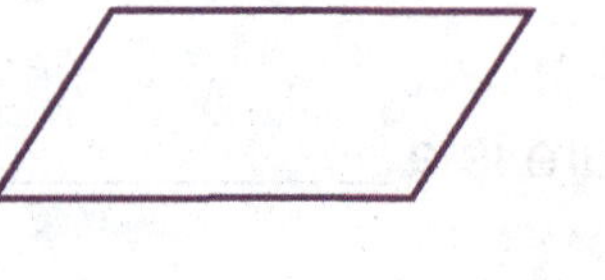

____

____

7. What shape is the traffic sign? ______________

For questions 8–11, draw each quadrilateral. Then classify it as a *parallelogram, rhombus, rectangle, square, or trapezoid.*

8. a rhombus with 4 right angles

____

9. a quadrilateral that has only 1 pair of parallel sides

____

10. a parallelogram with 4 equal sides

____

11. a parallelogram with 2 pairs of equal sides and 4 right angles

____

Solve each problem.

12. Rini designed a garden in the shape shown. What is the best name for the shape of the garden?

____

13. What is the best name for the shape of the window?

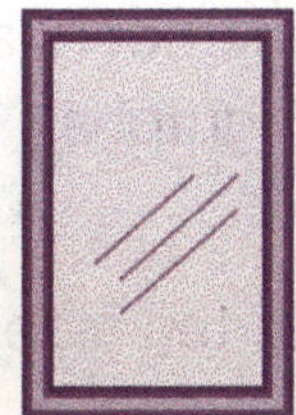

____

Glossary

acute triangle a triangle with three acute angles (less than 90°) (Page 36)

capacity the amount a container can hold (Page 4)

circle a plane figure with all points an equal distance from the center (Page 32)

coordinate plane a plane or grid formed by two intersecting and perpendicular lines called axes (Page 24)

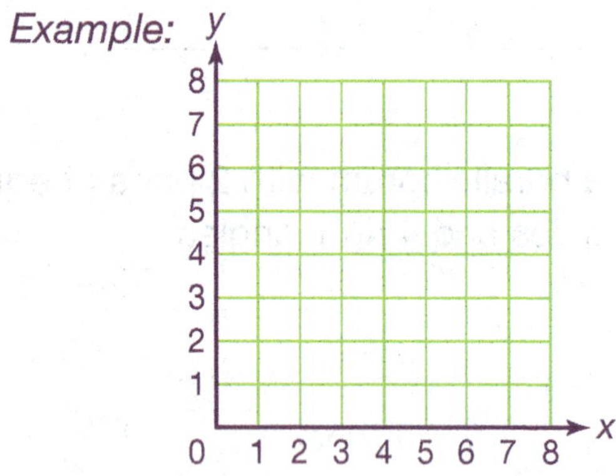

cube a solid figure with six congruent square faces (Page 16)

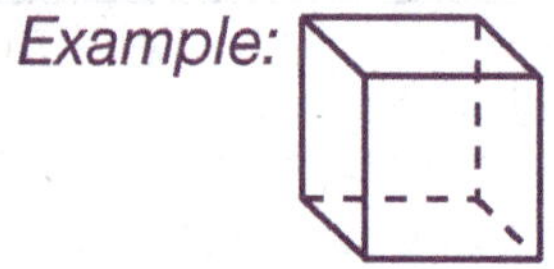

cubic unit a unit of volume with dimensions 1 unit × 1 unit × 1 unit (Page 12)

customary units standard units of measurement such as feet, pounds, and gallons (Page 4)

data information collected about people or things. Data that are numbers are often shown in tables or graphs. (Page 20)

decagon a polygon with ten sides and ten angles (Page 32)

equilateral triangle a triangle with three equal sides (Page 36)

gram (g) a metric unit for measuring mass (Page 8)

hexagon a polygon with six sides and six angles (Page 32)

isosceles triangle a triangle with two equal sides (Page 36)

length the measurement of how long or tall something is (Page 4)

line plot a graph that uses a number line and Xs or dots to show data (Page 20)

liter (L) a metric unit for measuring capacity (Page 8)

meter (m) a metric unit for measuring length (Page 8)

metric units units of measurement based on the metric system such as meters, grams, and liters (Page 8)

obtuse triangle a triangle with one obtuse angle (greater than 90°) (Page 36)

octagon a polygon with eight sides and eight angles (Page 32)

ordered pair a pair of numbers (*x*, *y*) used to locate a point on a coordinate plane (Page 24)

origin the point where the two axes meet on a coordinate plane; named by the ordered pair (0,0) (Page 24)

parallelogram a quadrilateral with two pairs of equal sides and two pairs of parallel sides (Page 40)

Example:

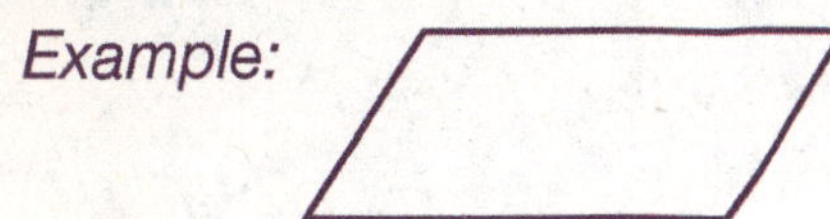

pentagon a polygon with five sides and five angles (Page 32)

plane figure a flat, two-dimensional figure such as a circle or rectangle (Page 32)

polygon a closed plane figure formed by three or more straight sides such as a triangle or rectangle (Page 32)

quadrilateral a plane figure with four straight sides (Page 40)

Example:

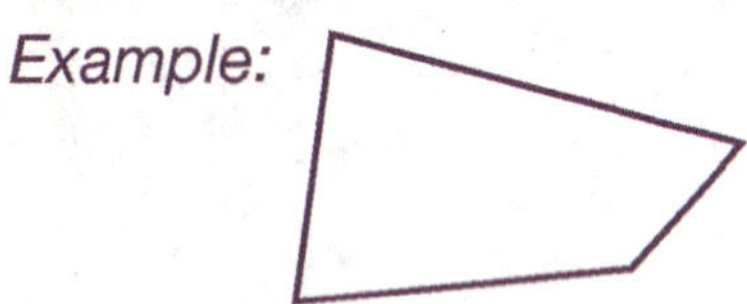

regular polygon a polygon with all equal sides and all equal angles such as a square (Page 32)

rectangle a polygon with four sides and four right angles (Pages 32, 40)

rectangular prism a solid figure in which all six faces are rectangles (Page 16)

Example:

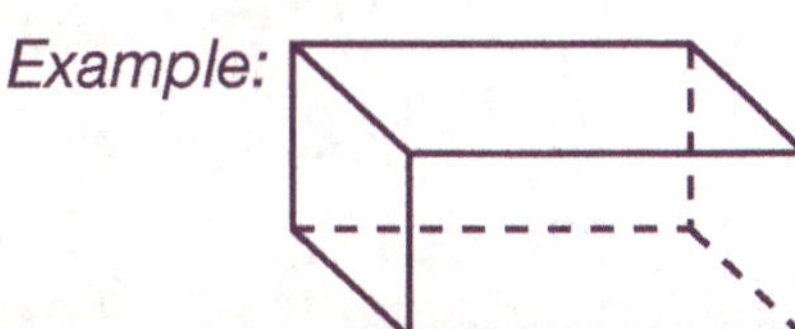

rhombus a quadrilateral with four equal sides and two pairs of parallel sides (Page 40)

right triangle a triangle with one right angle (Page 36)

scalene triangle a triangle with no sides equal (Page 36)

square a quadrilateral with four equal sides and four right angles (Page 40)

trapezoid a quadrilateral with exactly one pair of parallel sides (Page 40)

triangle a polygon with three sides and three angles (Pages 32, 36)

Example:

volume the amount of space enclosed by a solid figure (Pages 12, 16)

weight a measure of how heavy something is (Page 4)

***x*-axis** the left-right or horizontal number line on a coordinate plane (Page 24)

***x*-coordinate** the first number in an ordered pair (x, y) (Page 24)

***y*-axis** the up-down or vertical number line on a coordinate plane (Page 24)

***y*-coordinate** the second number in an ordered pair (x, y) (Page 24)

Math Tools: Customary Measurement Tables

Units of Length
1 foot (ft) = 12 inches (in.)
1 yard (yd) = 3 feet or 36 inches
1 mile (mi) = 1,760 yards or 5,280 feet

Units of Capacity
1 cup (c) = 8 fluid ounces (fl oz)
1 quart (qt) = 2 pints or 4 cups
1 gallon (gal) = 4 quarts

Units of Weight
1 pound (lb) = 16 ounces (oz)
1 ton (T) = 2,000 pounds

Math Tools: Metric Measurement Tables

Metric Units of Length
1 centimeter (cm) = 10 millimeters (mm)
1 meter (m) = 1,000 millimeters
1 meter = 100 centimeters
1 kilometer (km) = 1,000 meters

Metric Units of Capacity
1 liter (L) = 1,000 milliliters (mL)
1 kiloliter (kL) = 1,000 liters

Metric Units of Mass
1 gram (g) = 1,000 milligrams (mg)
1 kilogram (kg) = 1,000 grams